Stress Relieving Summer Designs

Adult Coloring Book

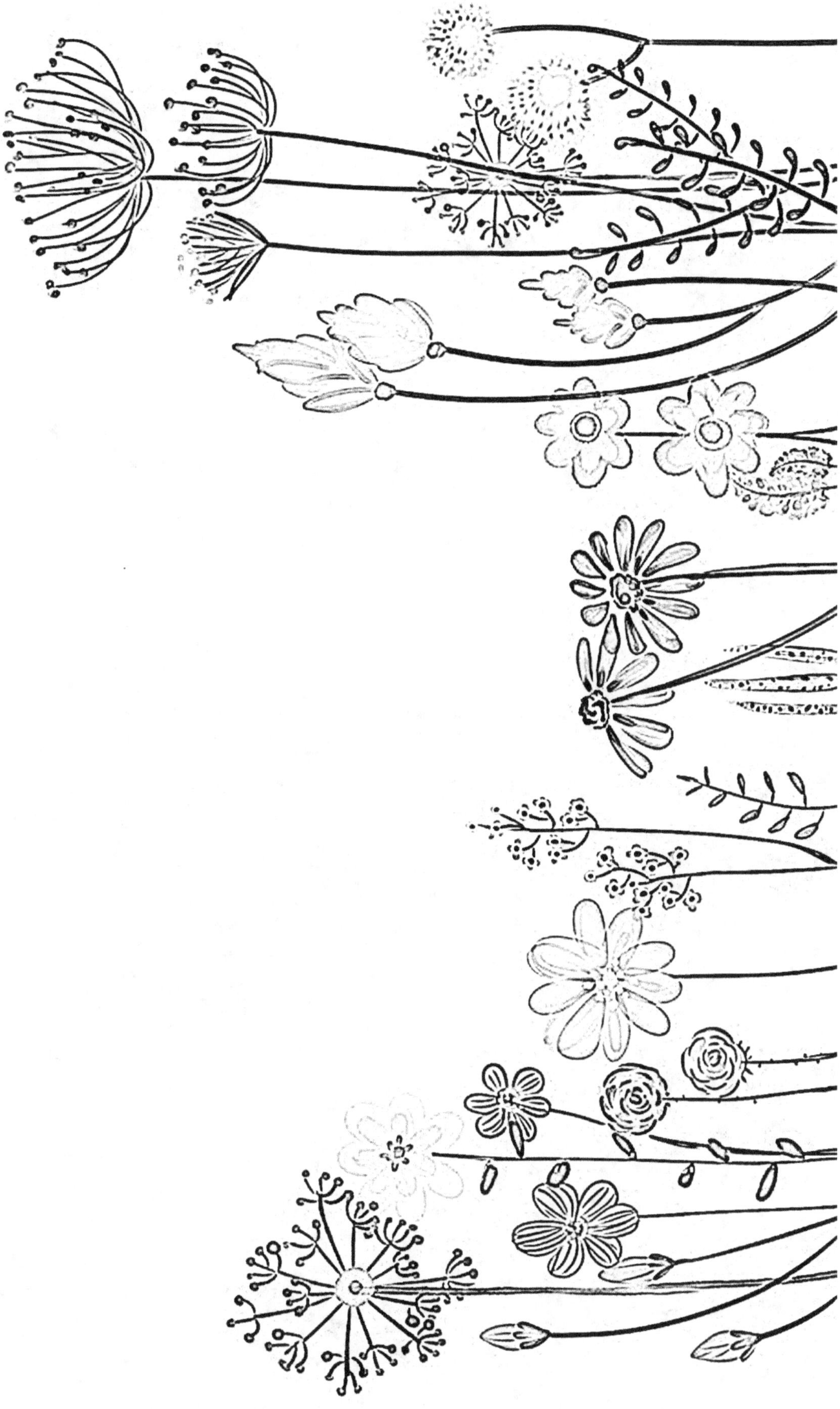

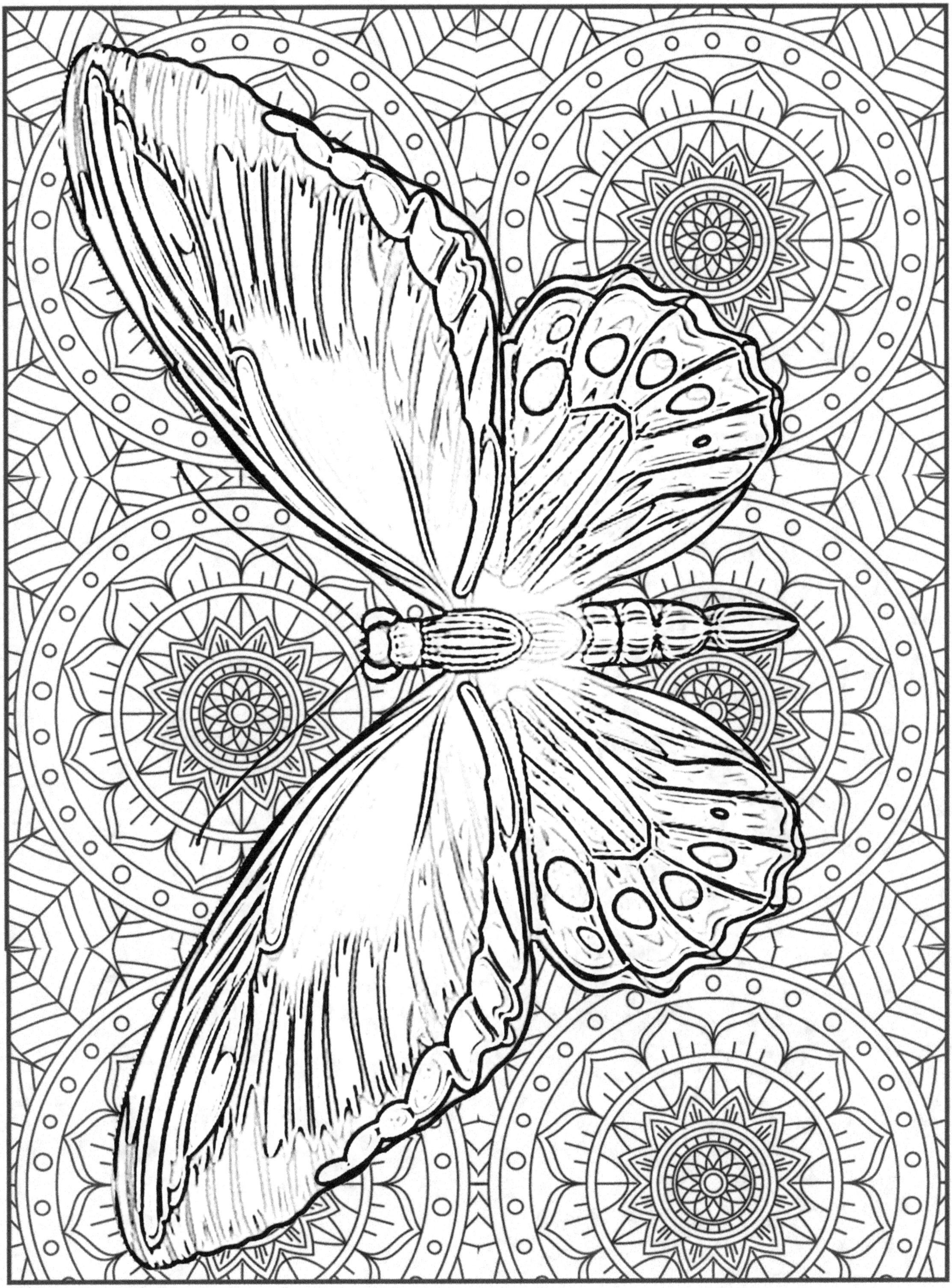

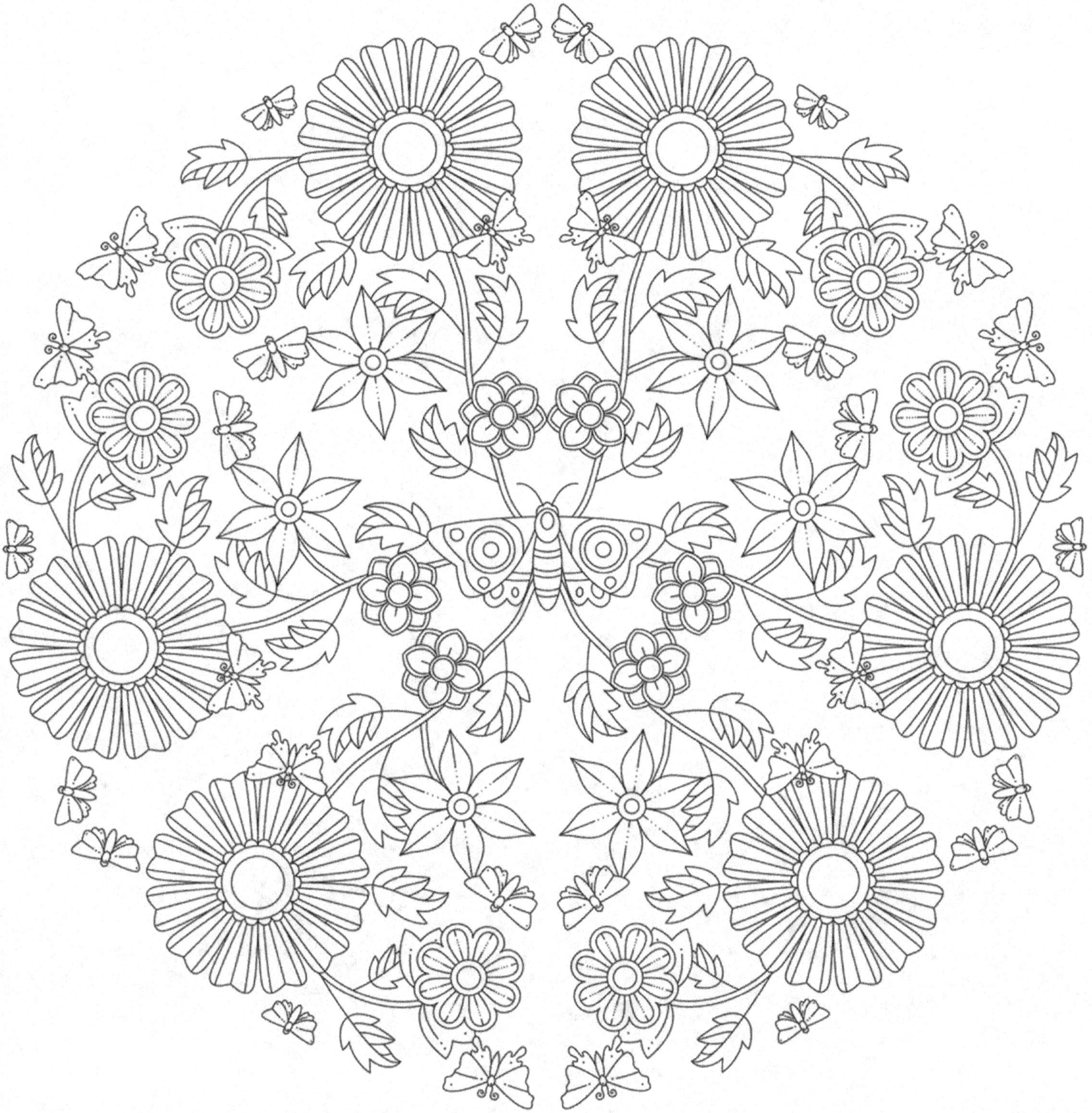

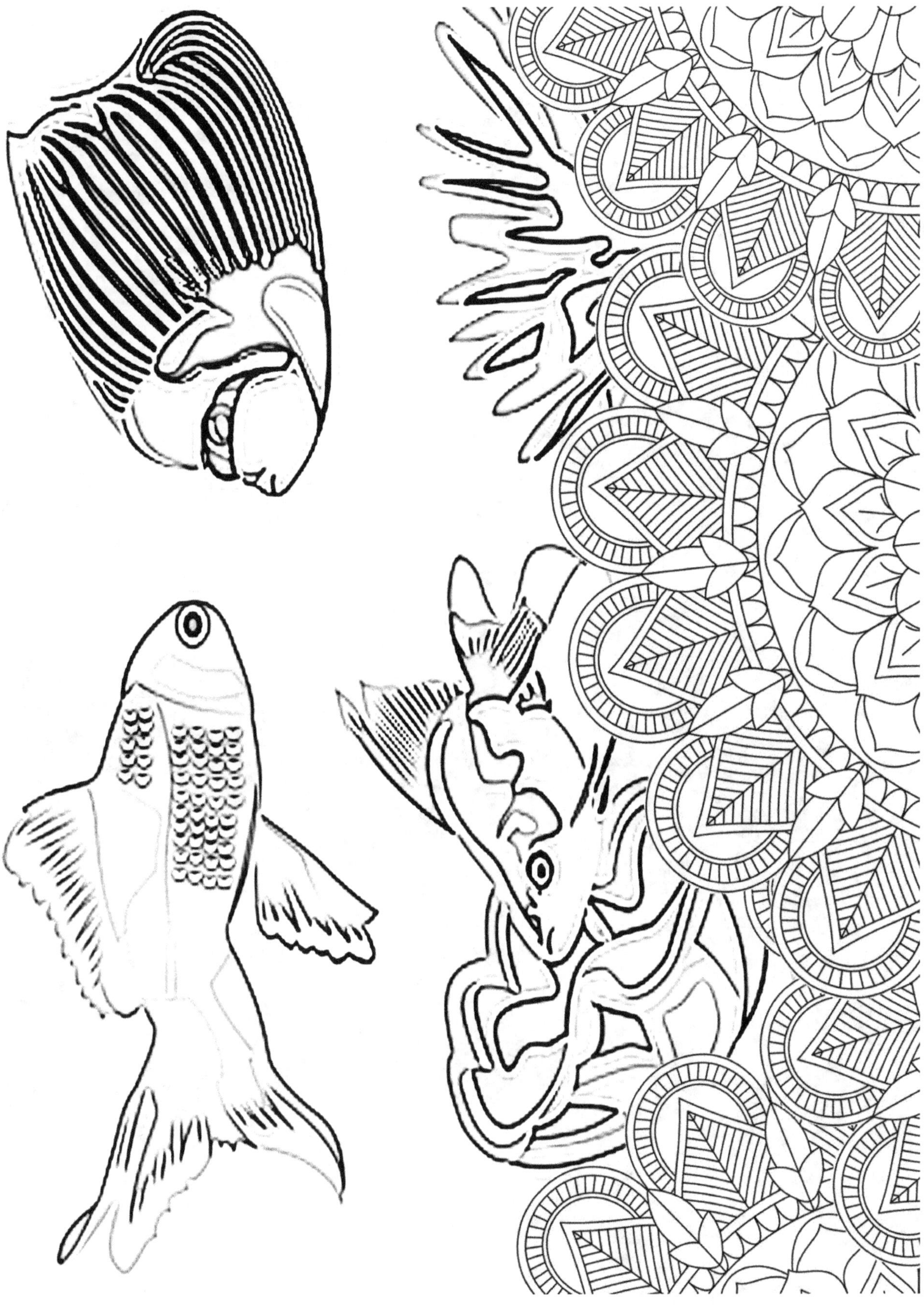

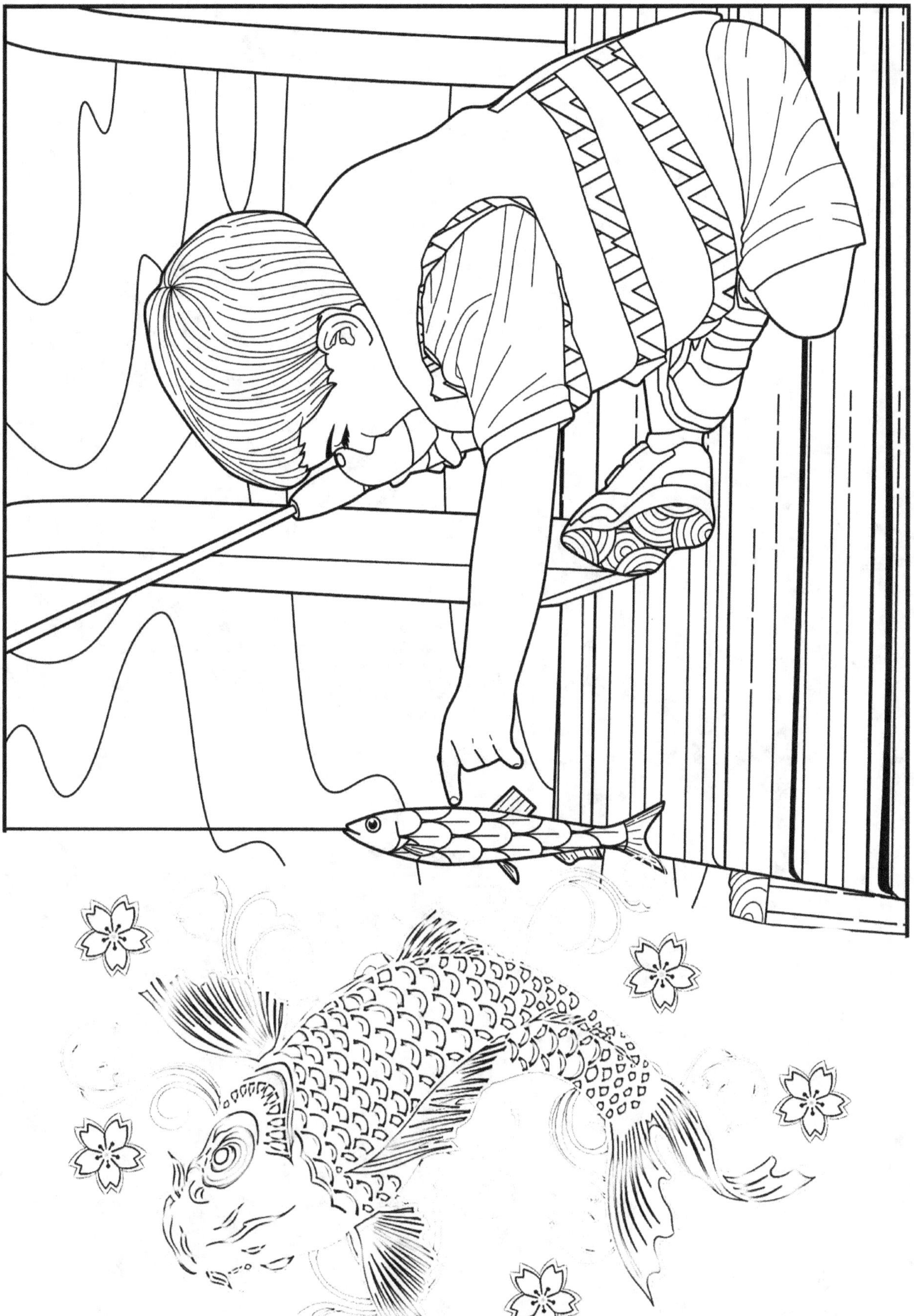

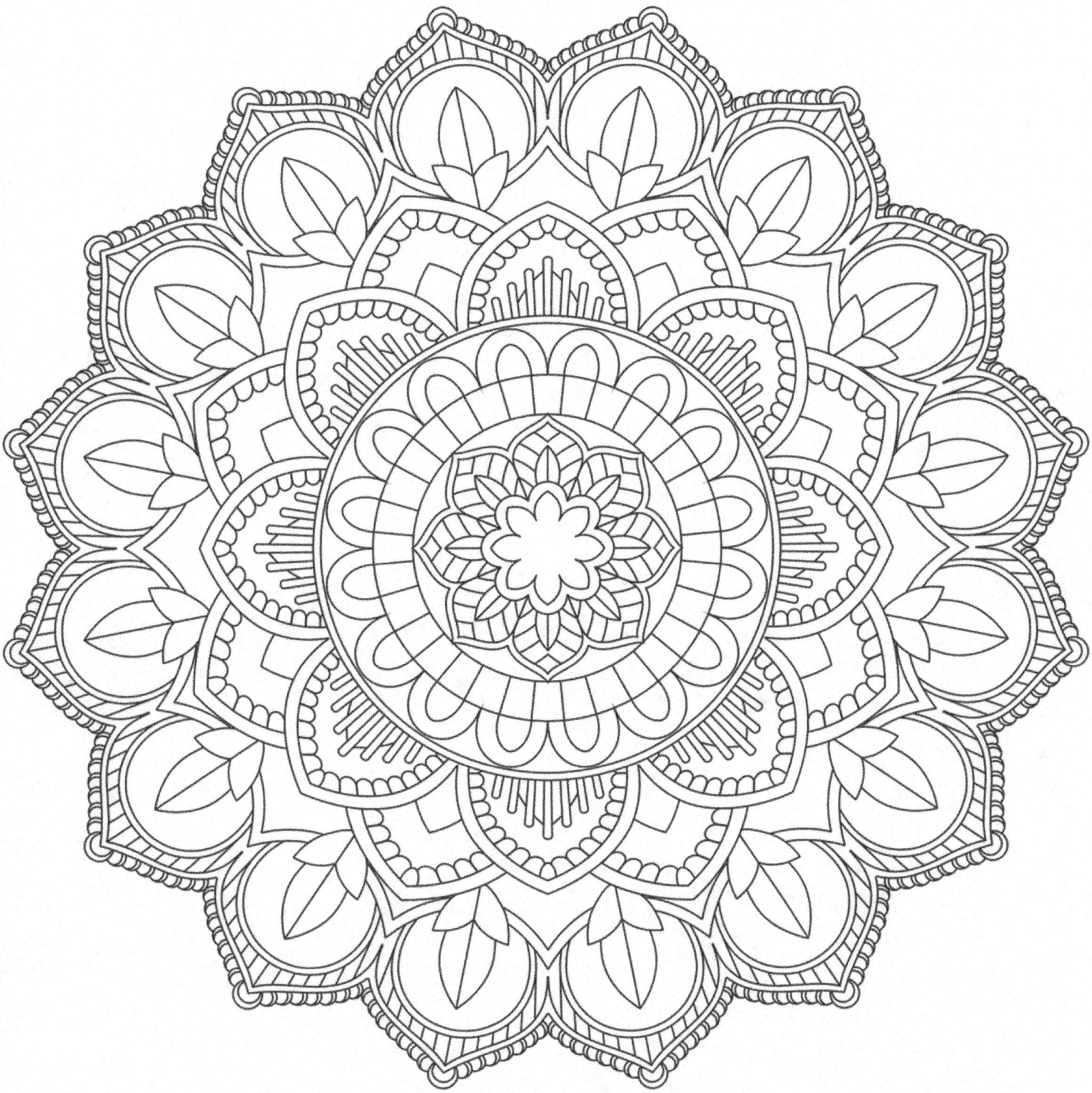

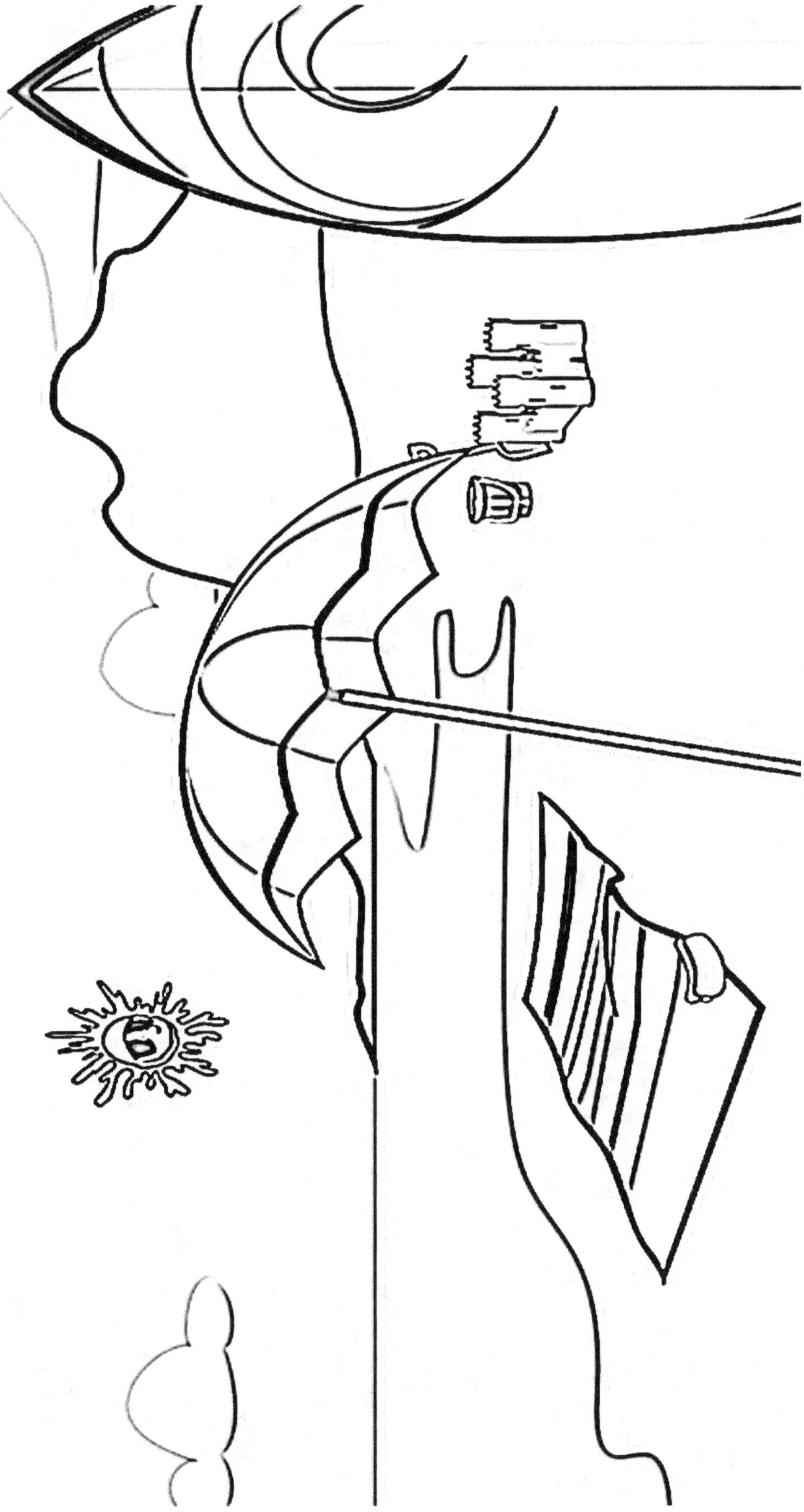

At the end of the day, the goals are simple: safety and security.

-Jodi Rell

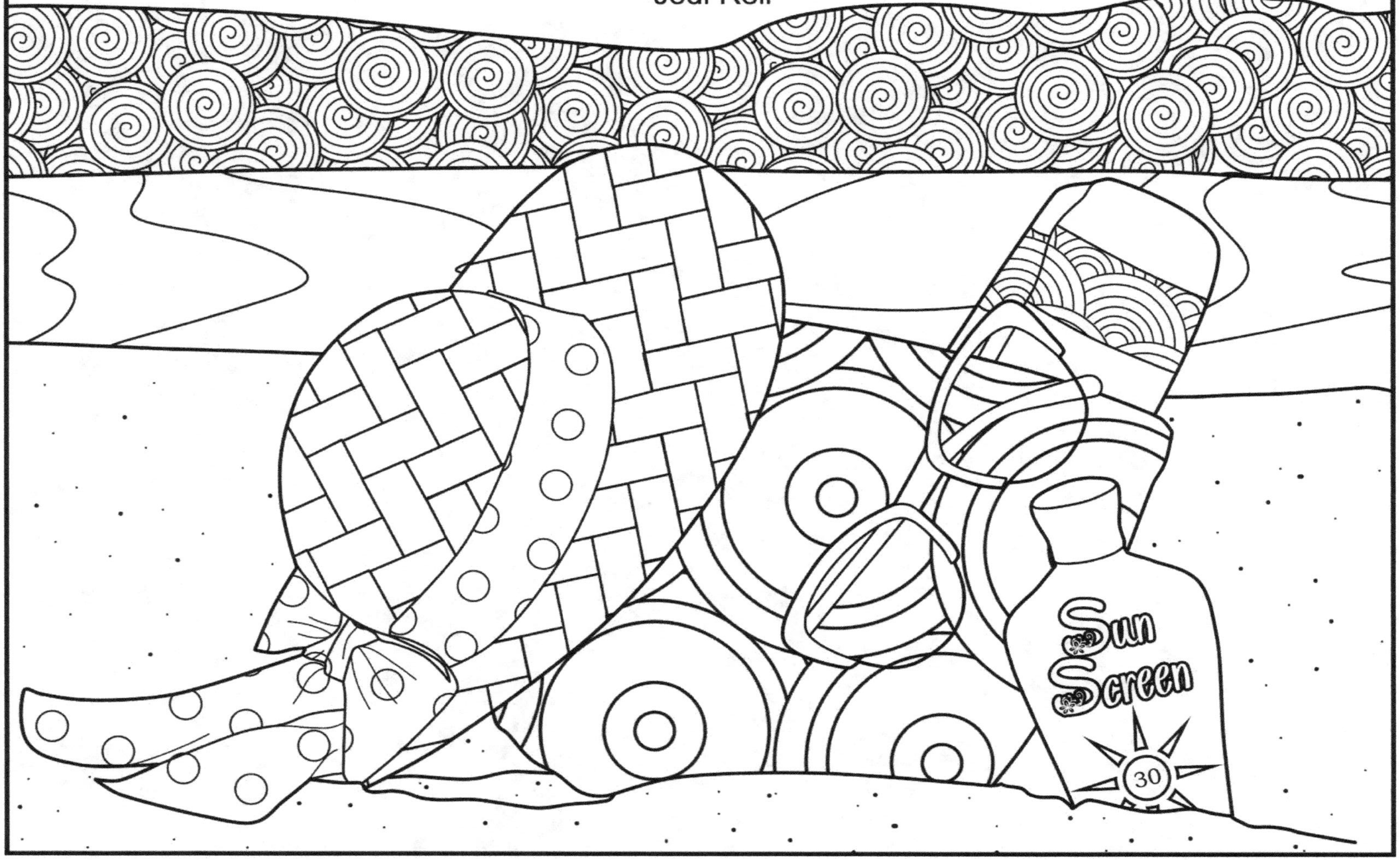

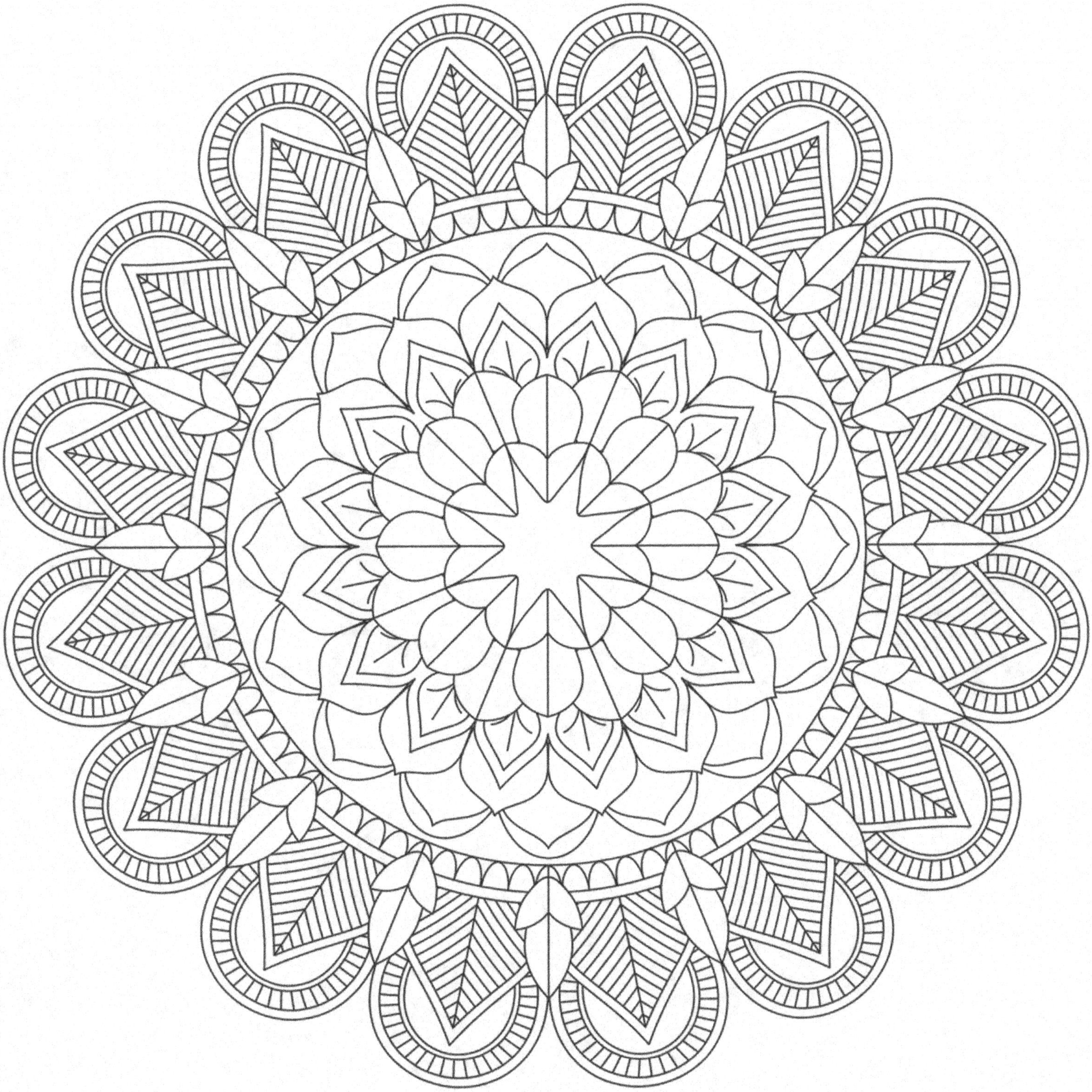

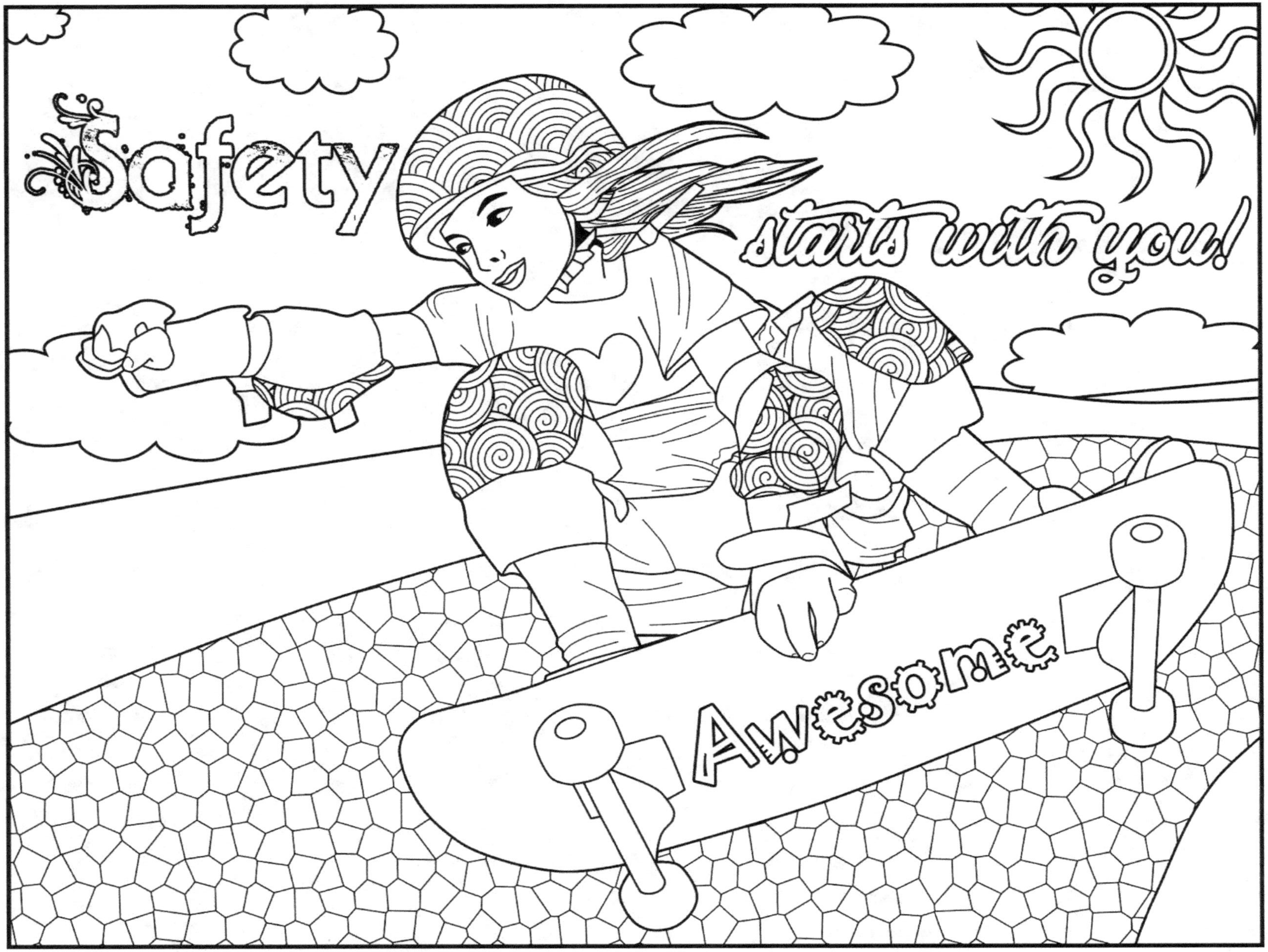
Safety
starts with you!
Awesome

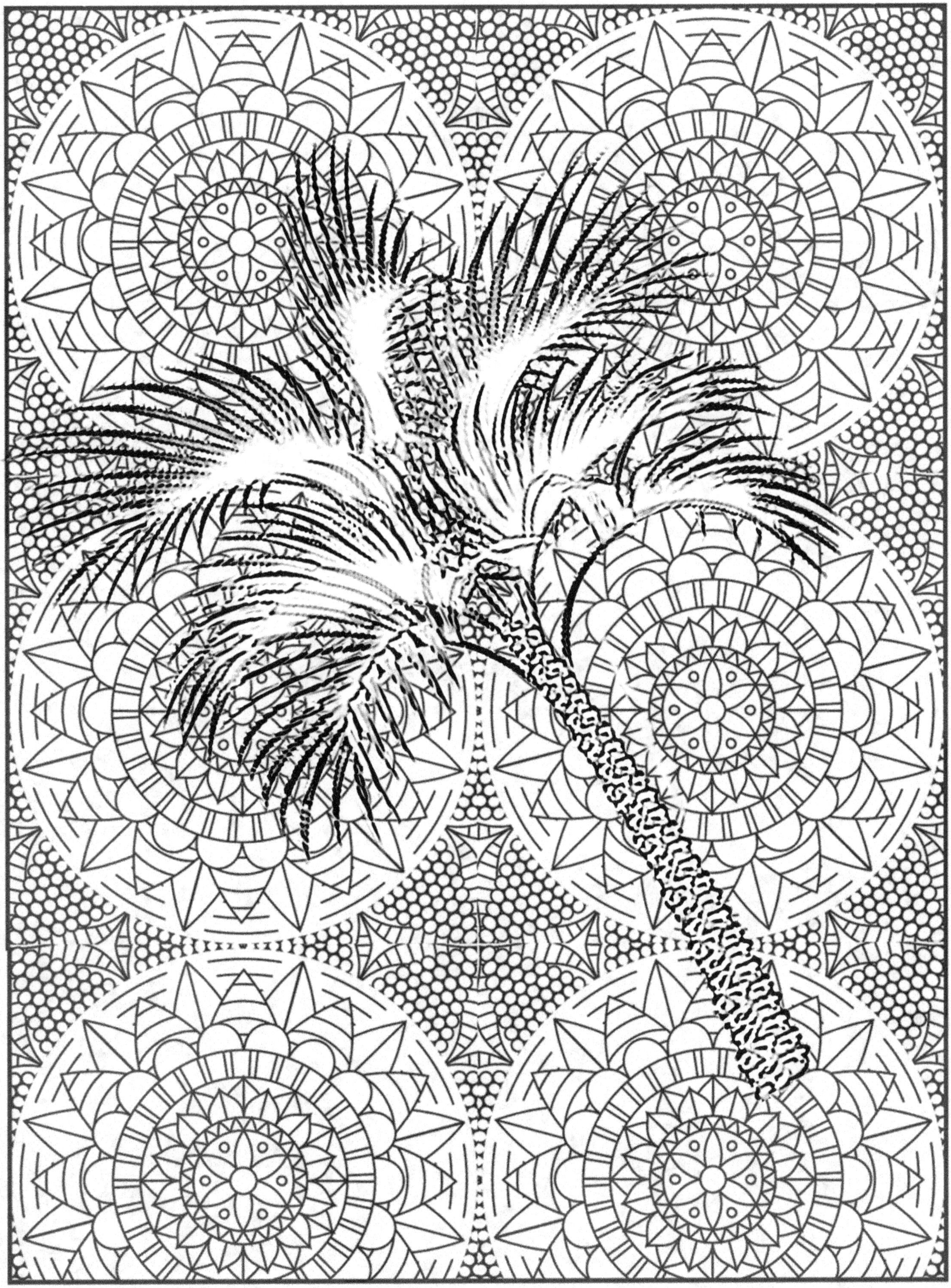

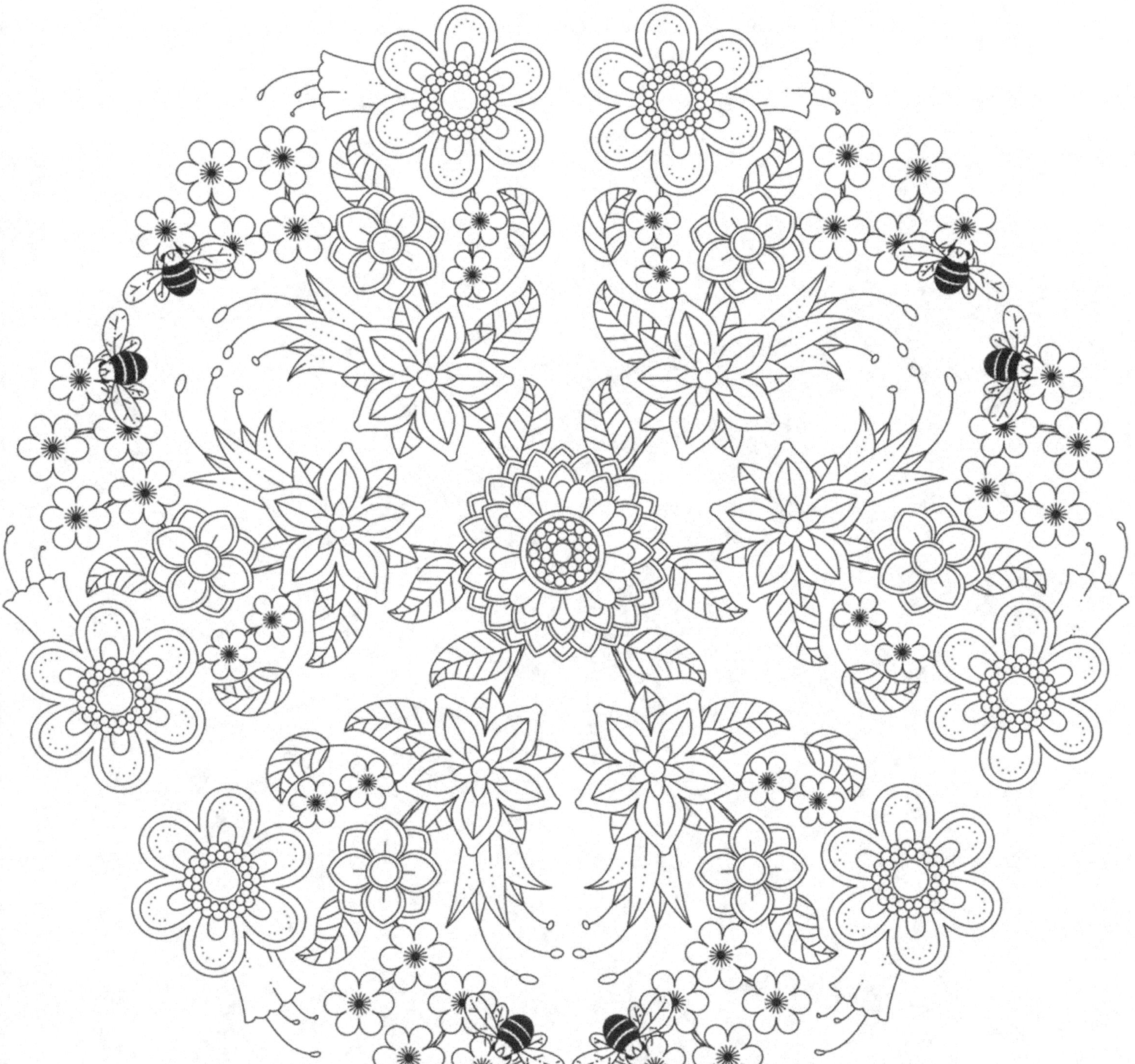

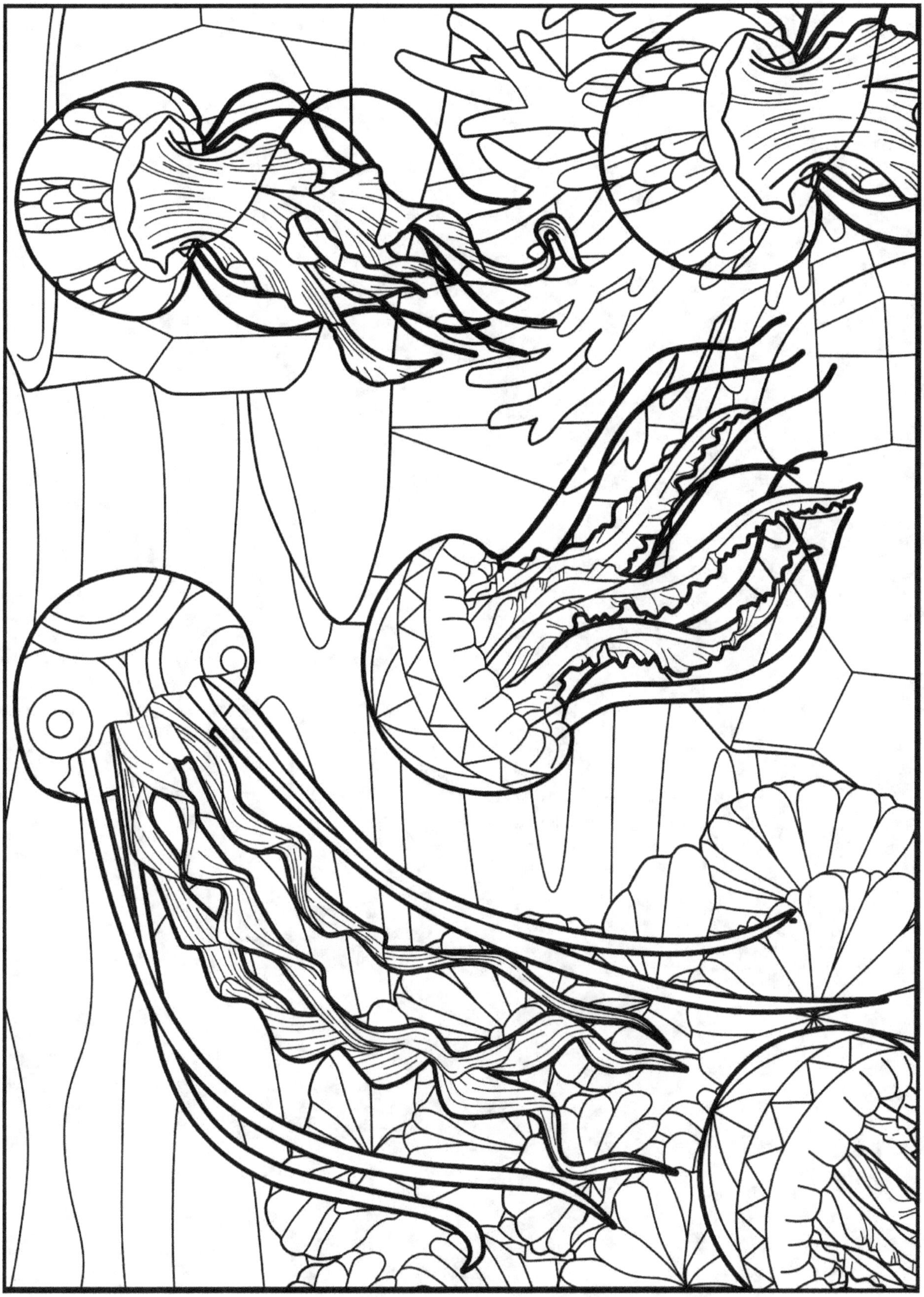

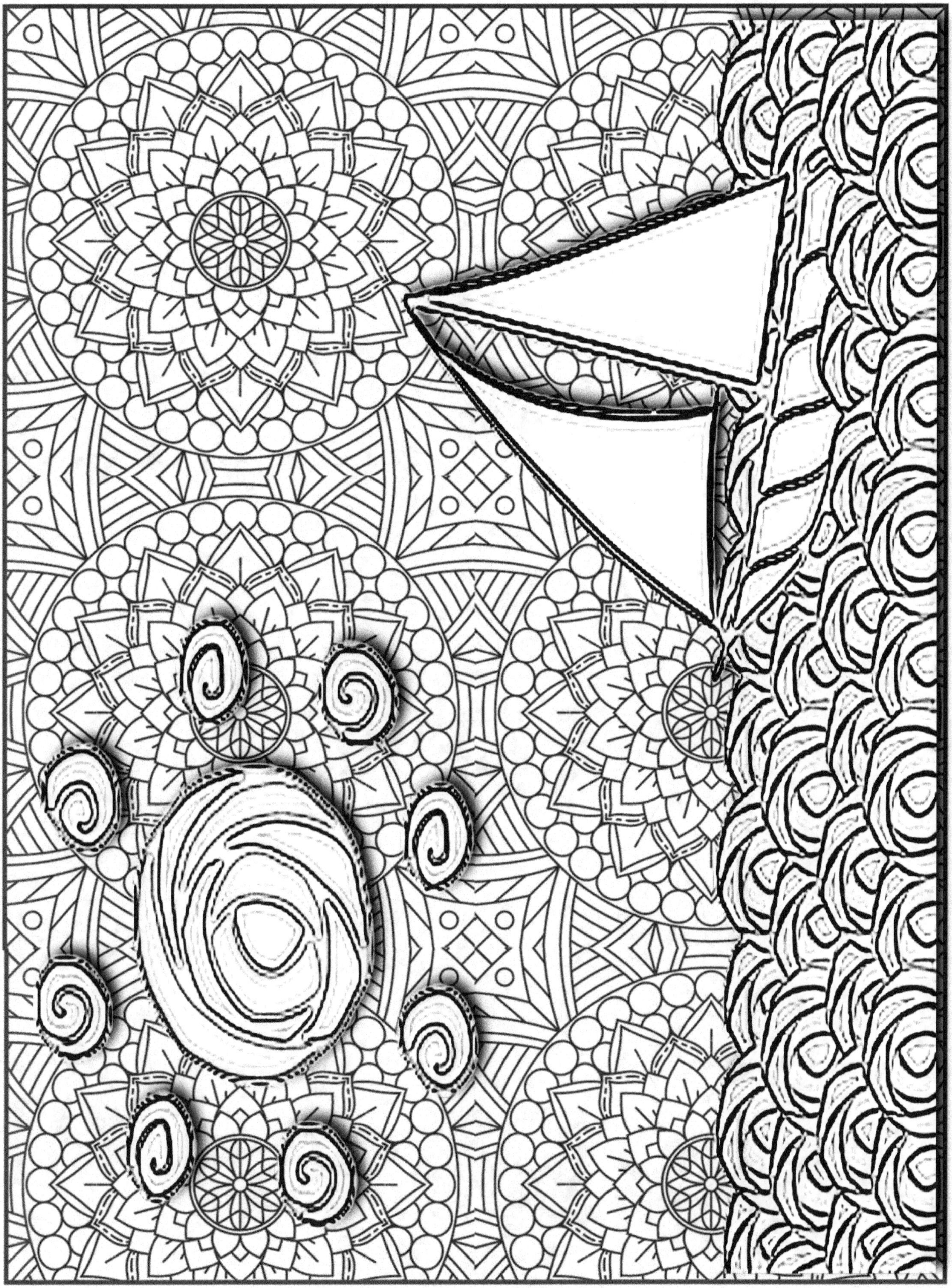

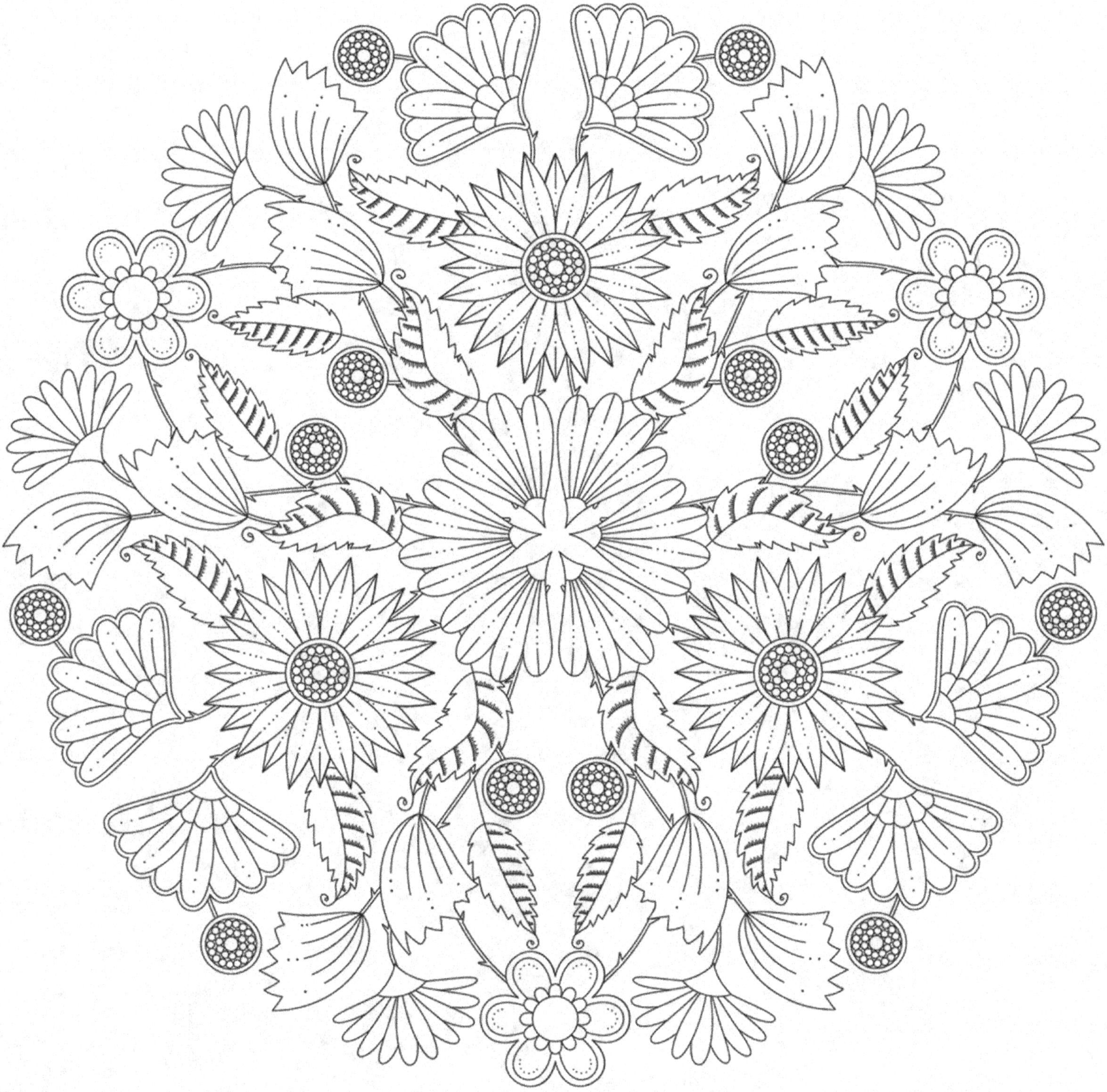

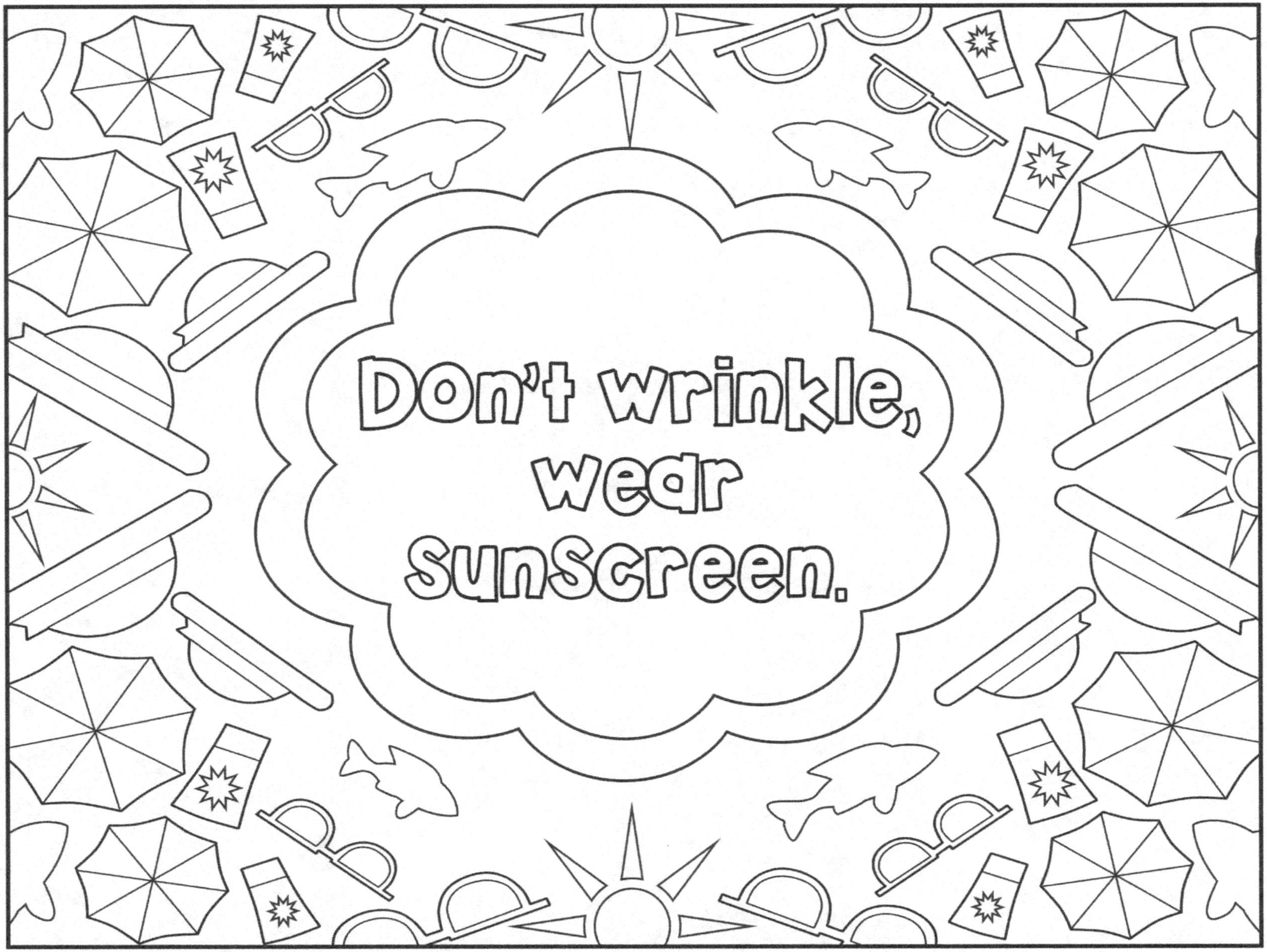
Don't wrinkle,
wear
sunscreen.

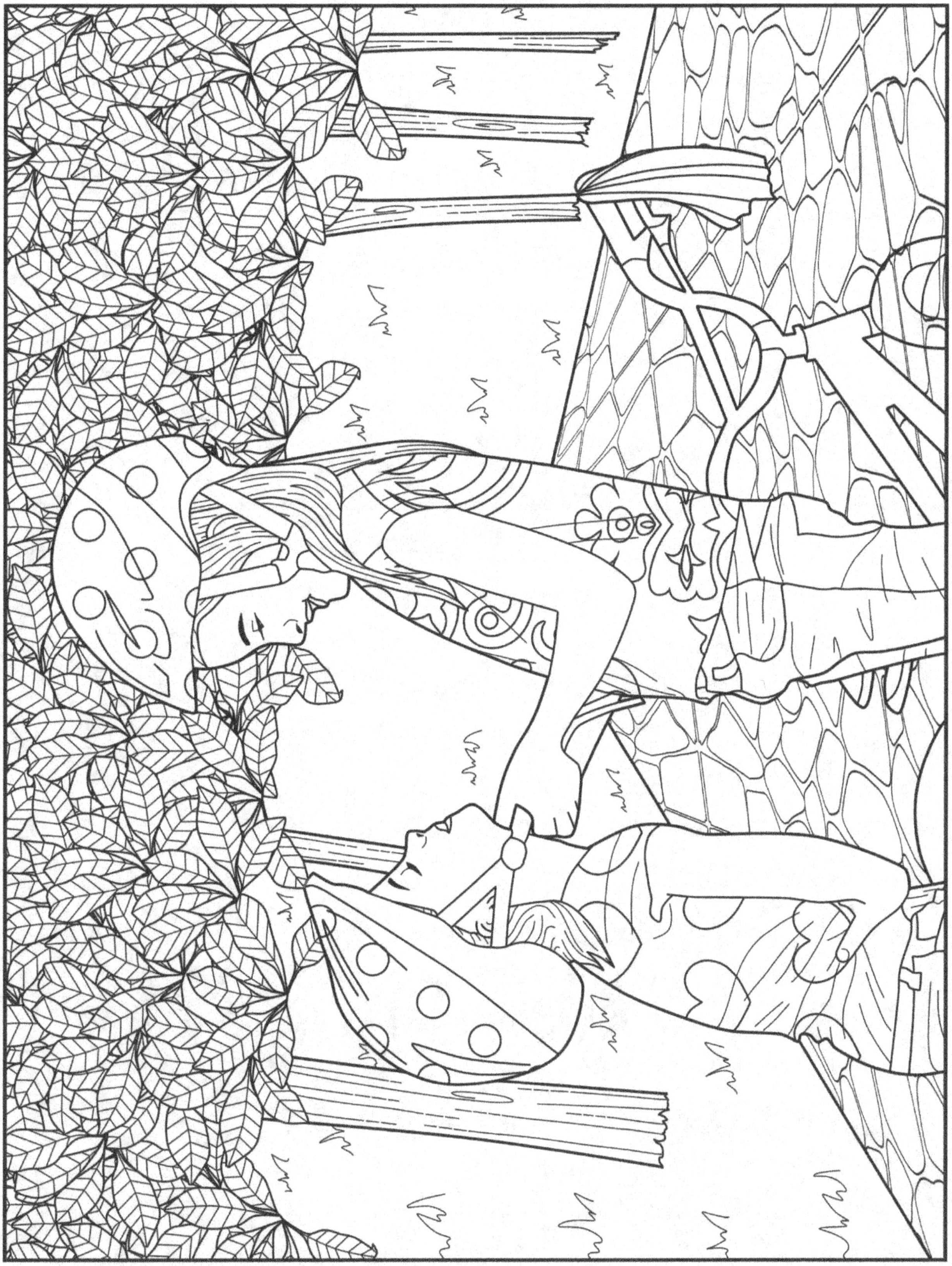

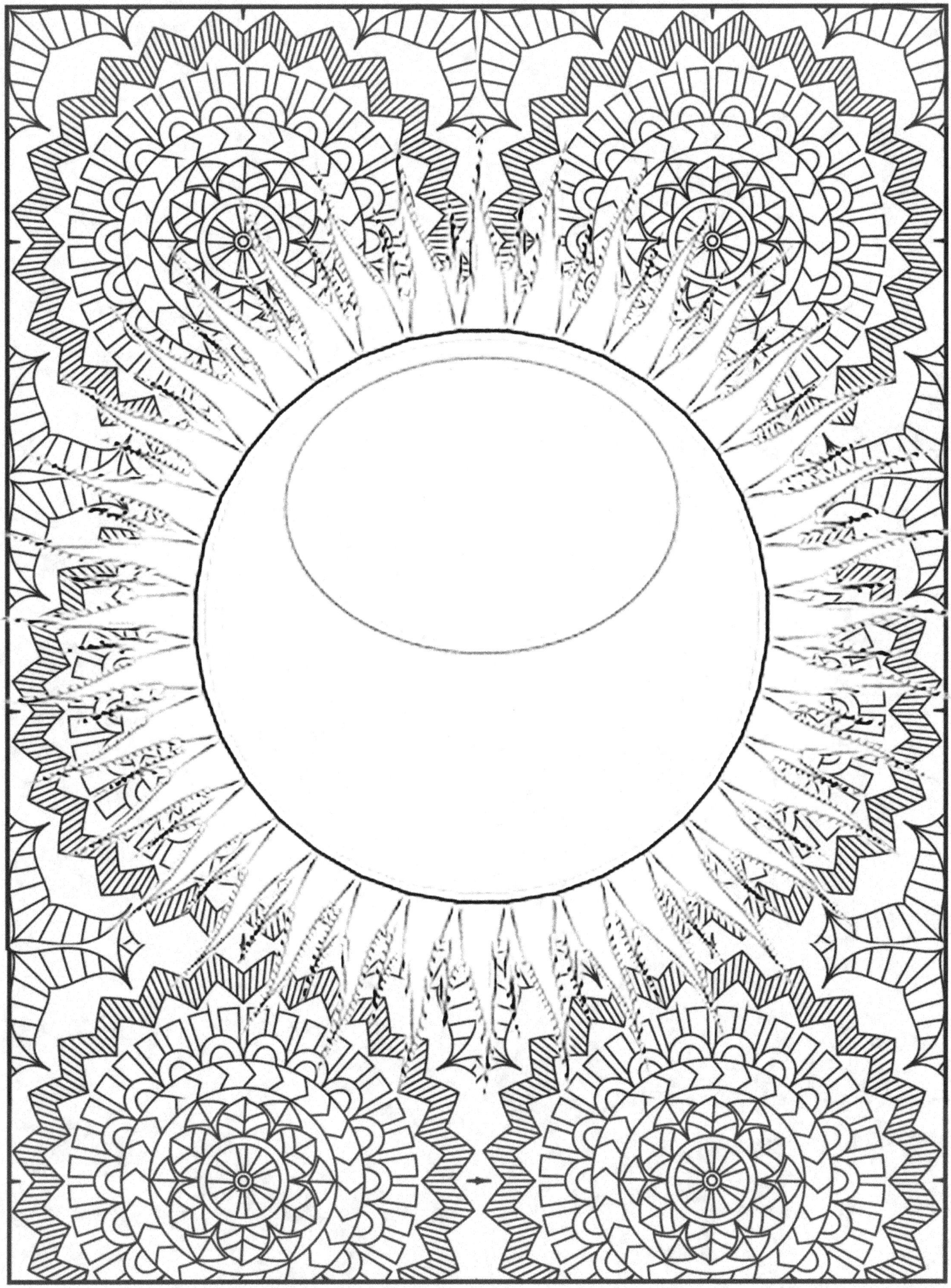

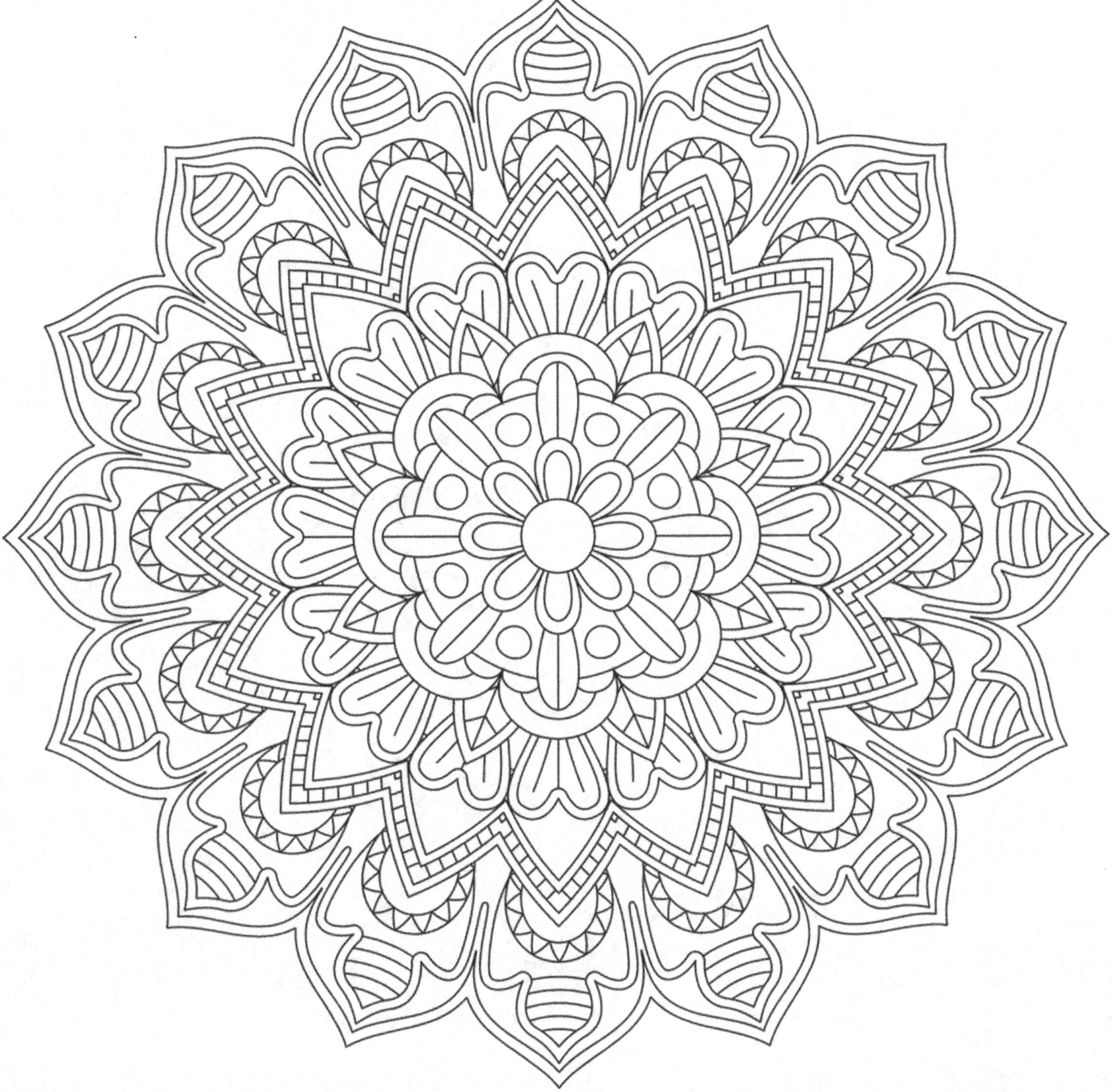

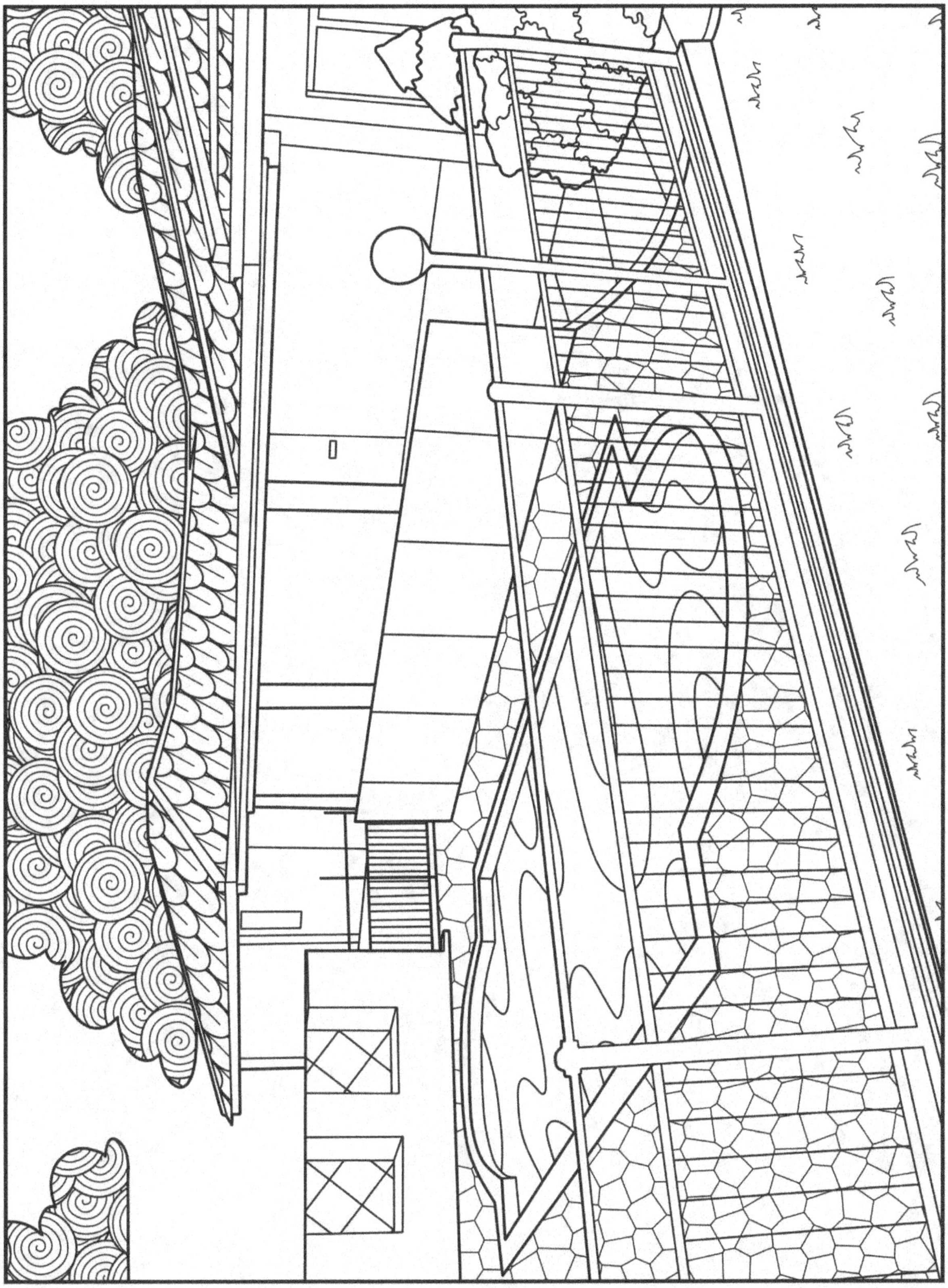

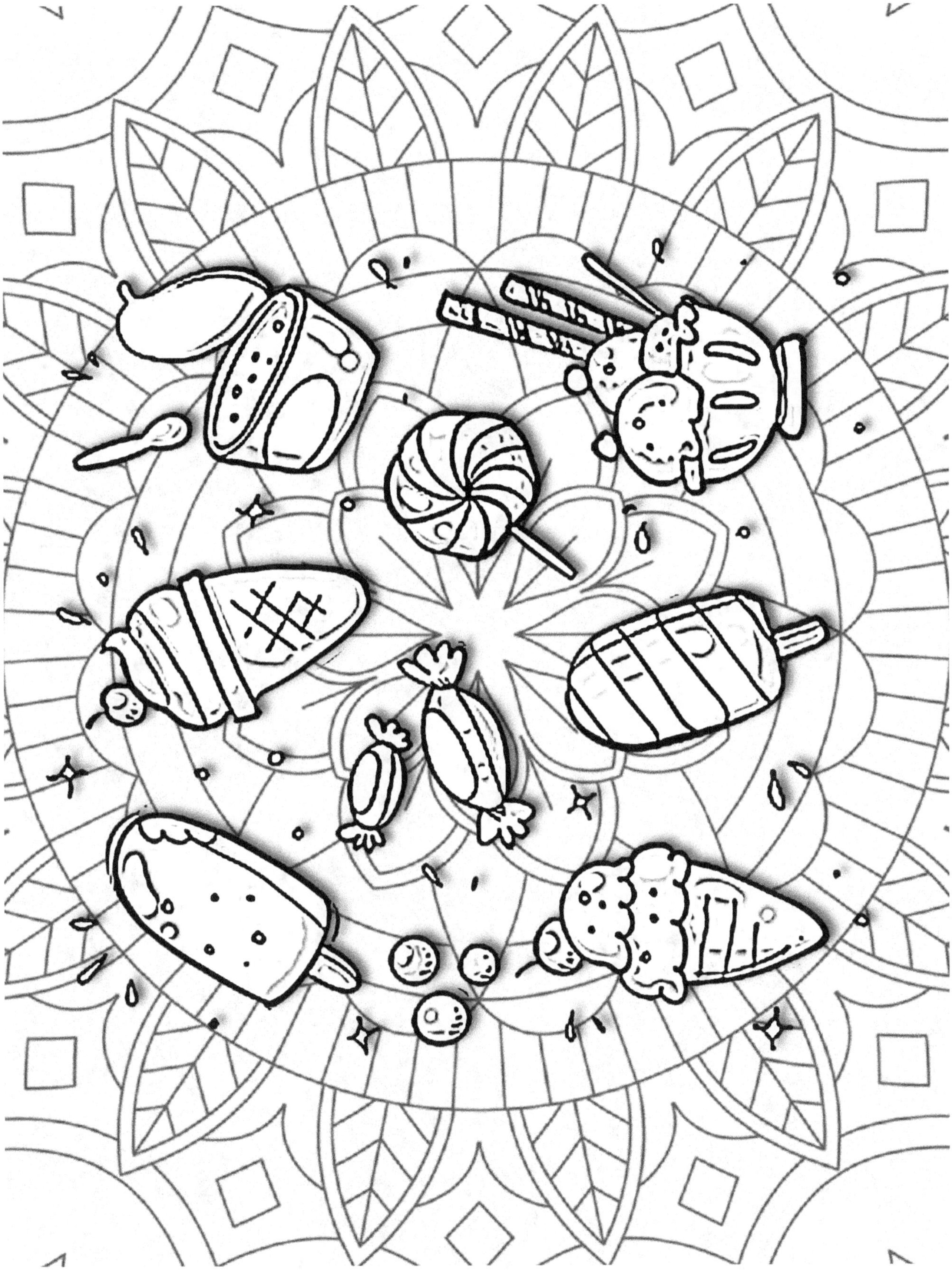

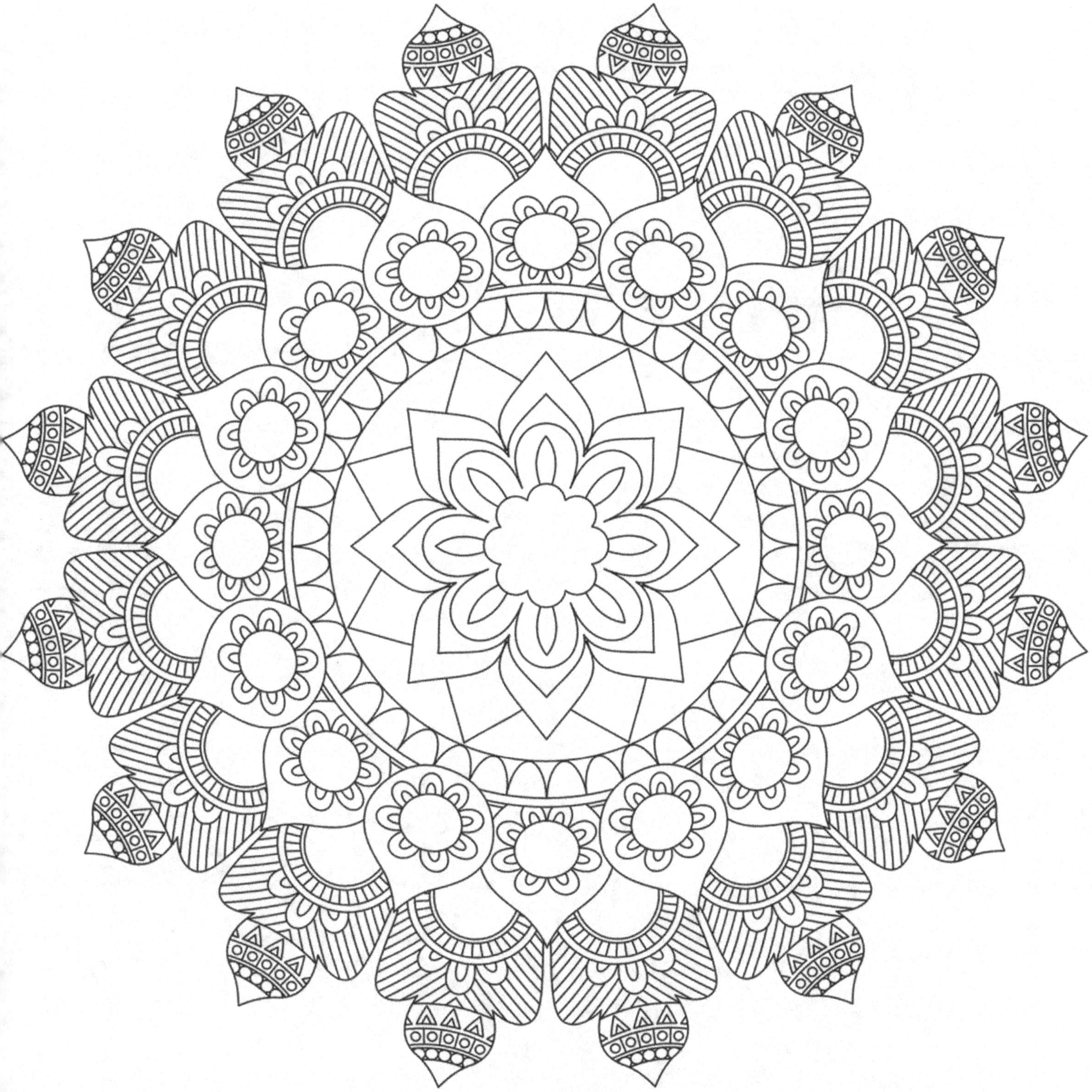

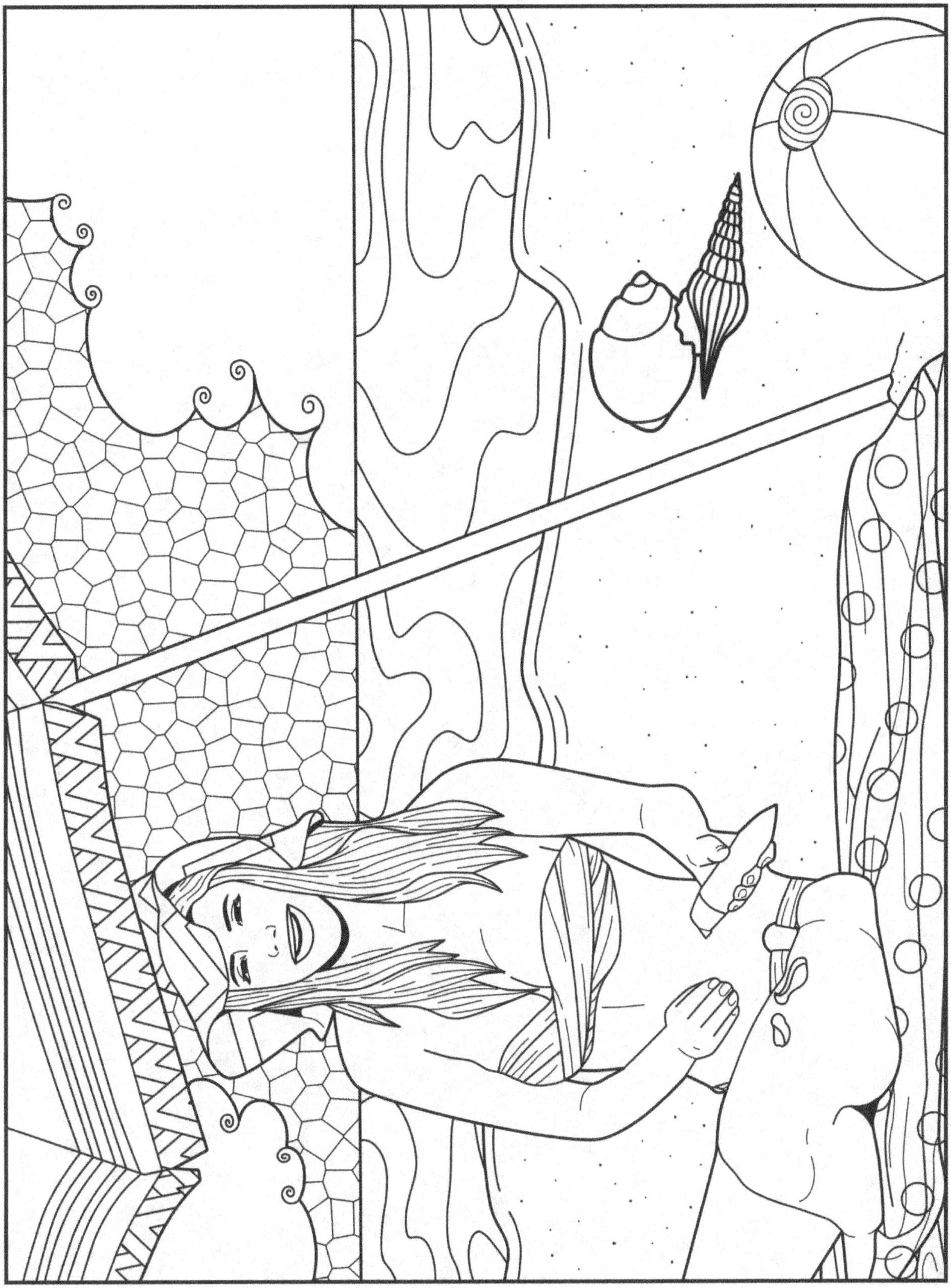

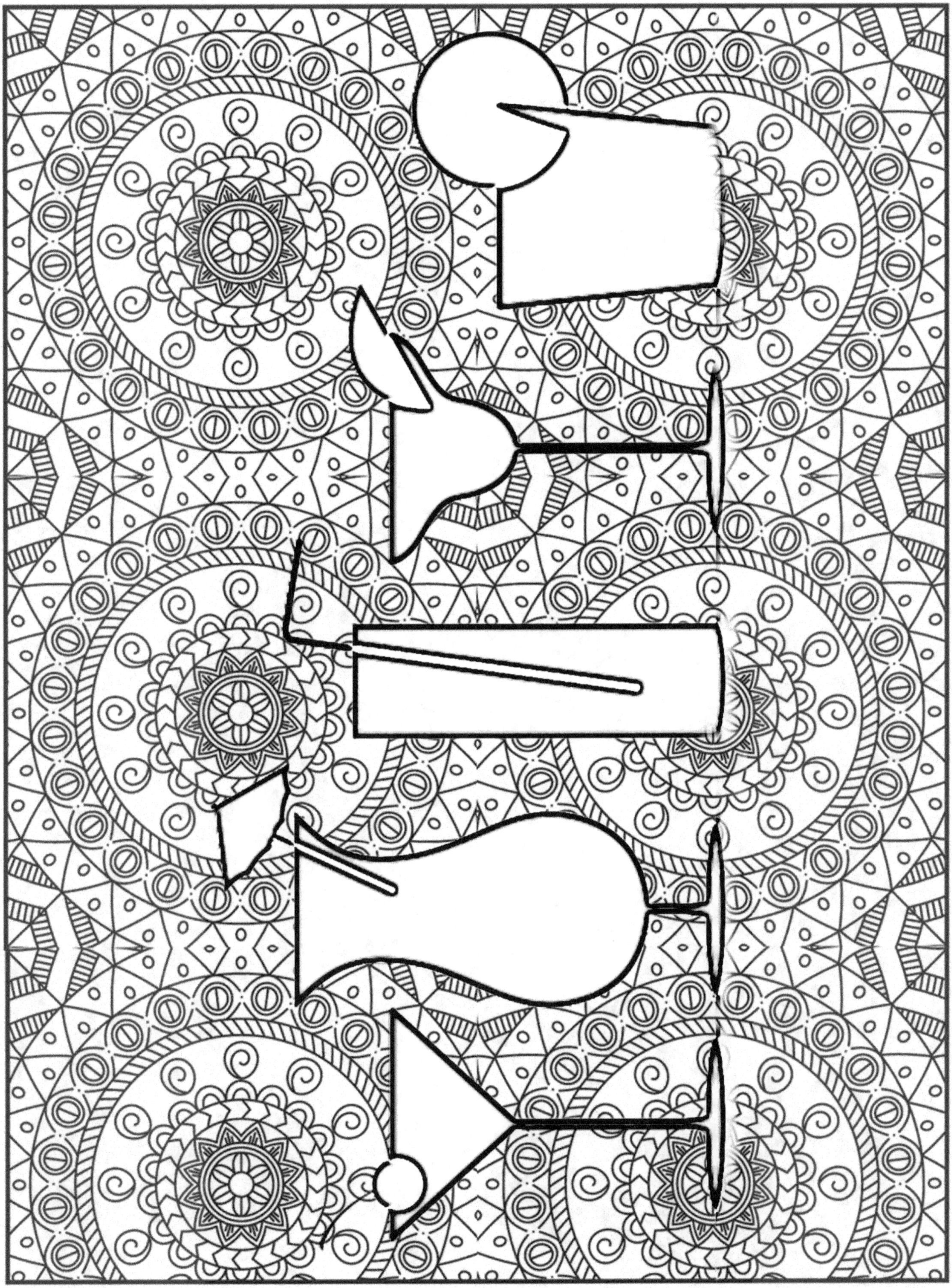

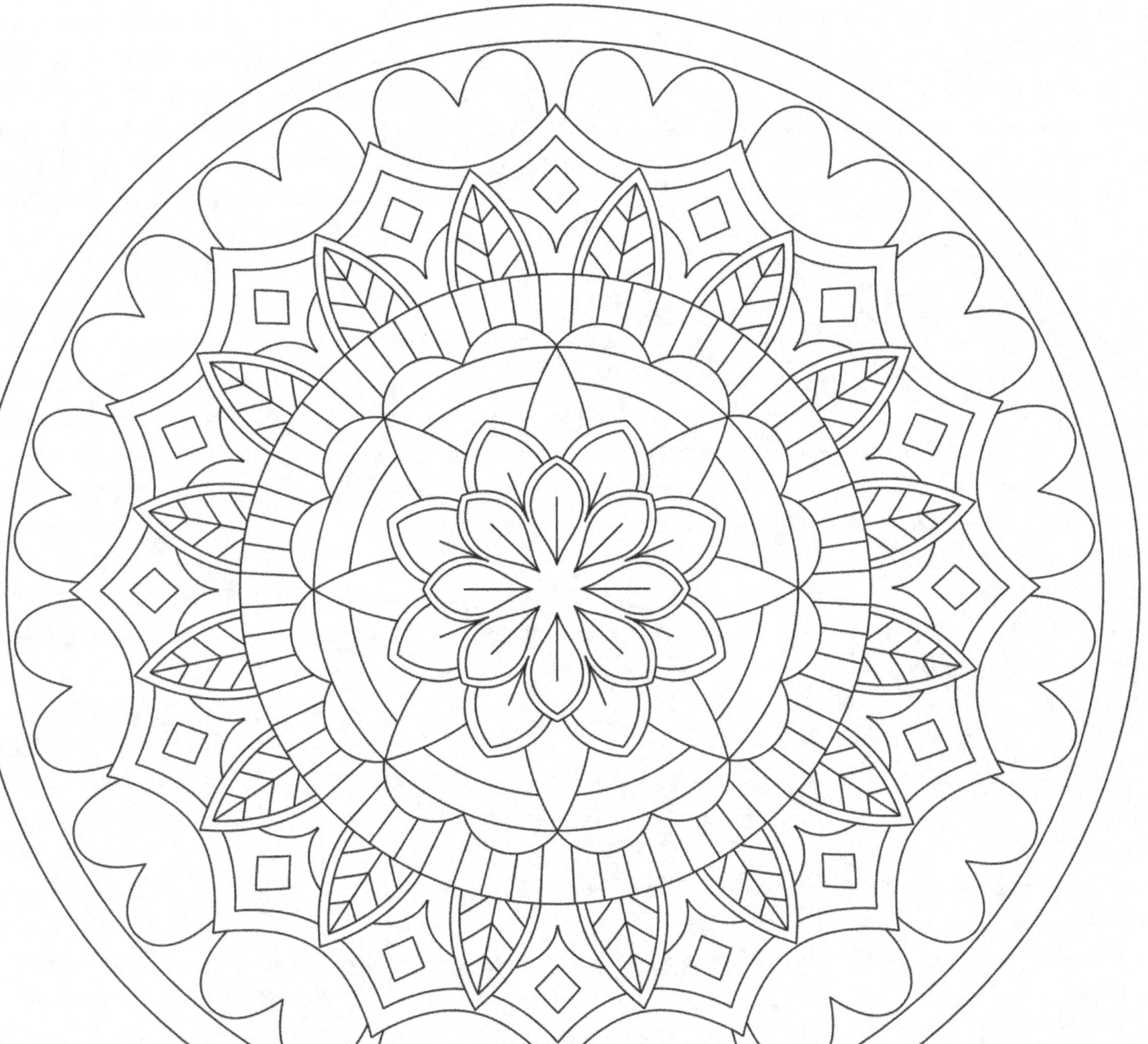

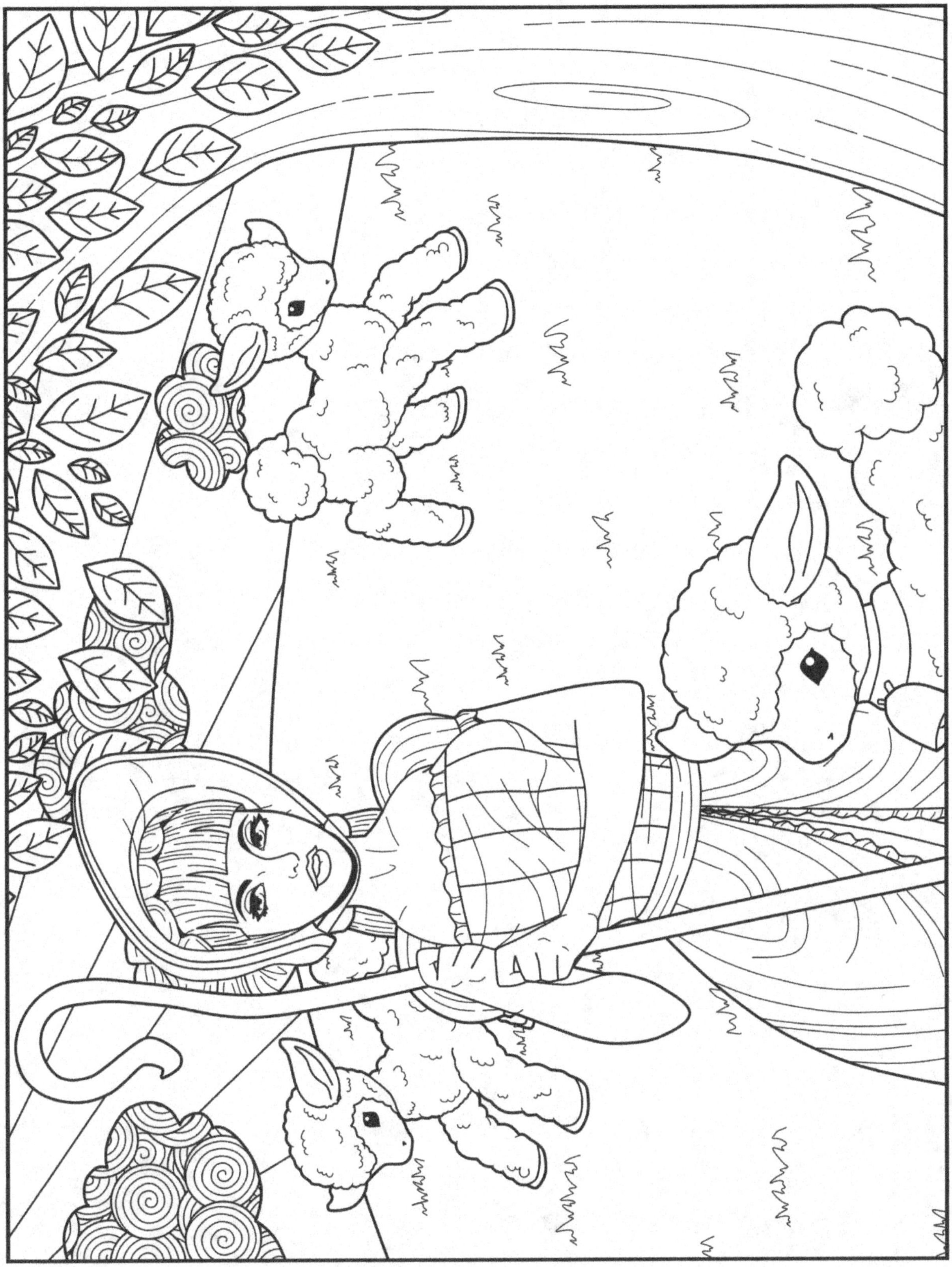

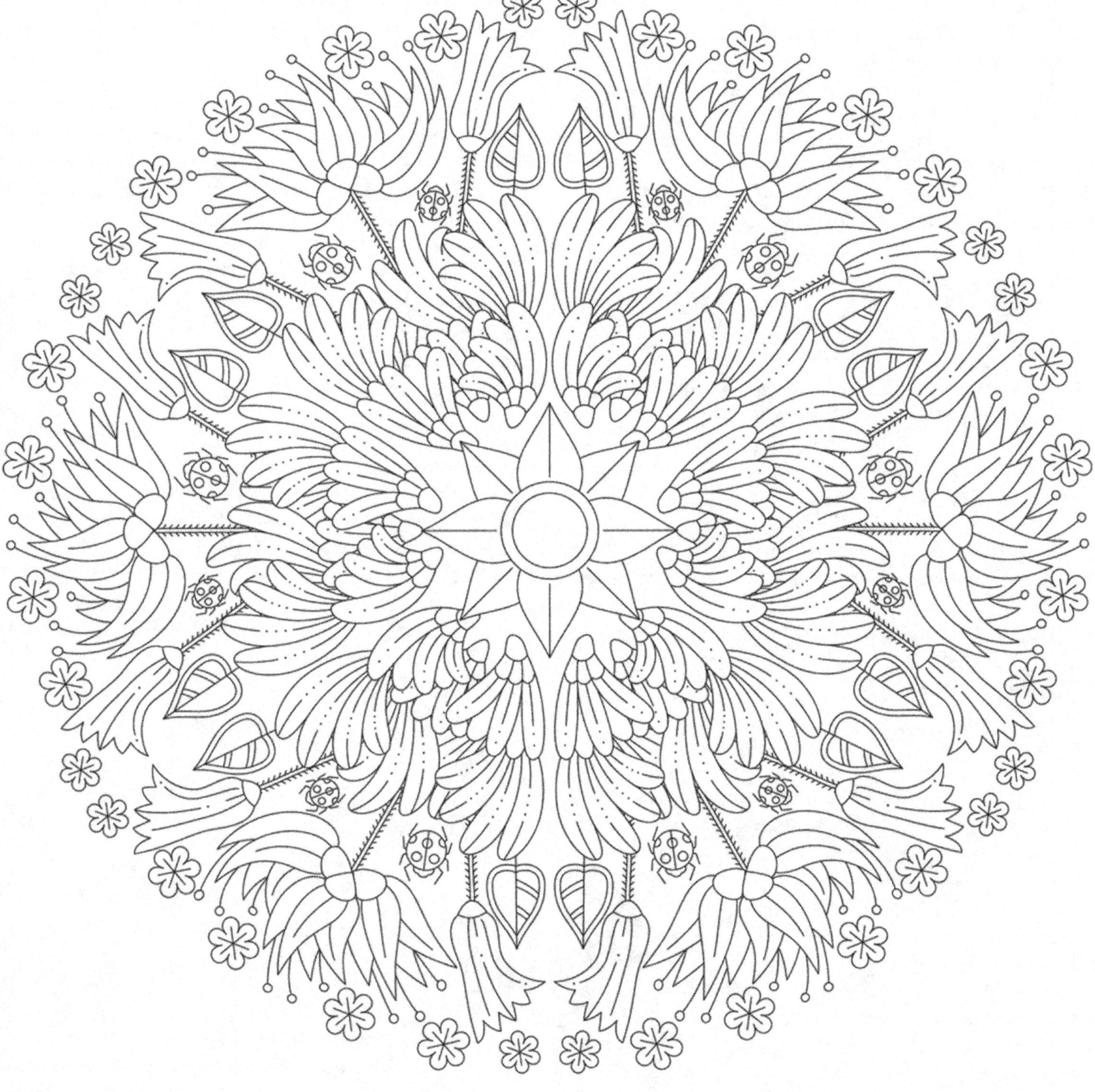

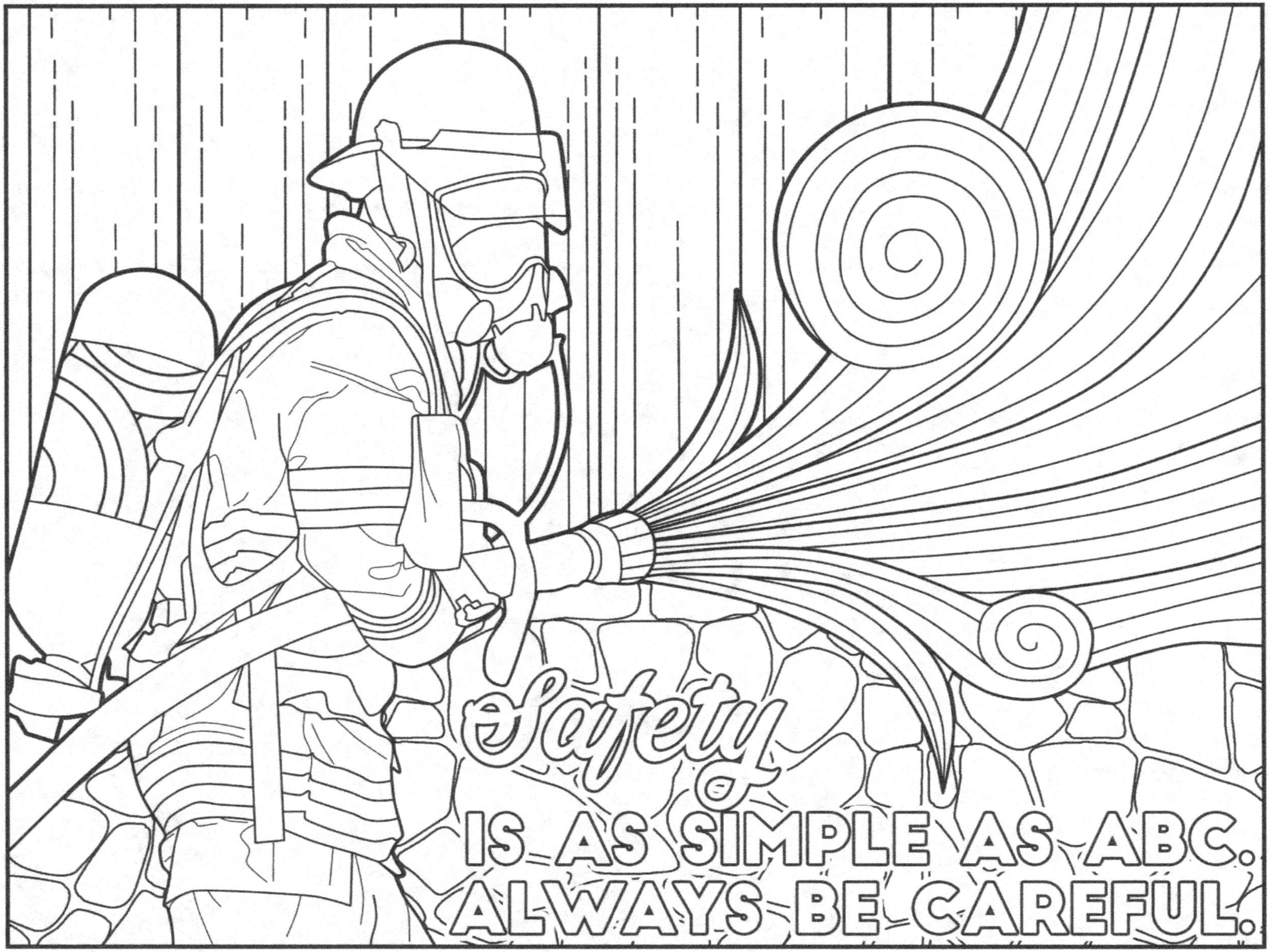
Safety
IS AS SIMPLE AS ABC.
ALWAYS BE CAREFUL.

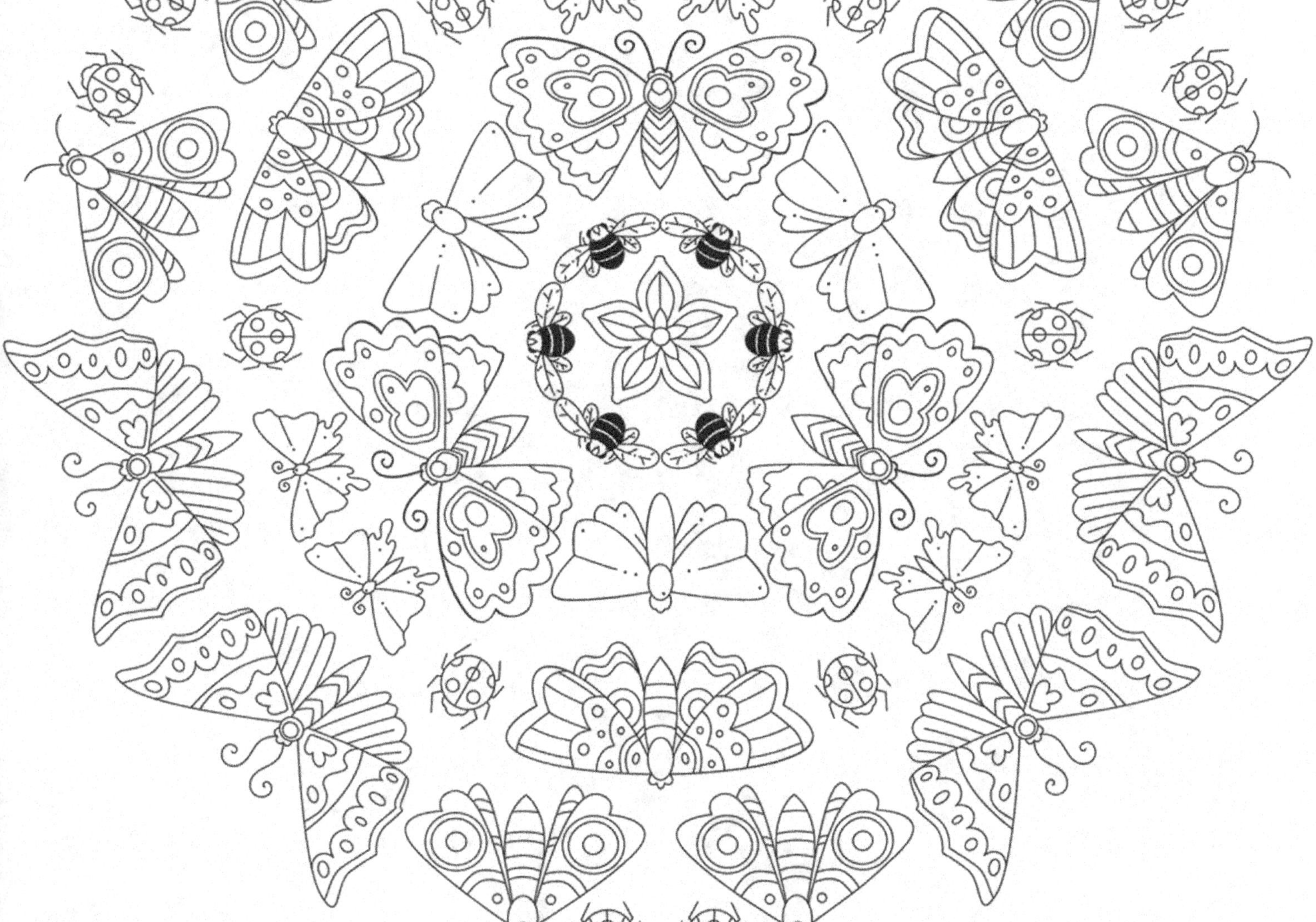

www.ingramcontent.com/pod-product-compliance
Lightning Source LLC
Chambersburg PA
CBHW081257180526
45170CB00007B/2466
9780359659883